Stay & Play Together

A Couples Guide To Longevity

Stay & Play Together

A Couples Guide To Longevity

BY

TRACY WILSON

Published by
Beautiful Publications LLC
Stratford, CT 06614

©Copyright 2023 Tracy Wilson

LIBRARY OF CONGRESS CONTROL NUMBER:
2023903319

HARDCOVER ISBN: 979-8-9855290-2-9
PAPERBACK ISBN: 978-1-7356620-3-9
EBOOK ISBN: 978-1-7356620-2-2

Printed in the United States of America

Contents

PART TWO

PLAY TOGETHER

AFTERWORD

INTRODUCTION

I've been married to my best friend for 23 years and I've been in a relationship with him for 41 years.

I met my husband in 1982 when I was 19 years old. 18 years later, we got married. 23 years later with 4 adults and 3 grandchildren, we're still married. We're best friends, we still love each other, and we're still in love with each other. Let me repeat that: We're best friends, we still love each other, and we're still in love with each other.

Our children called us 'Love Birds' when they were younger. When they got to Junior High School & High School, their friends would always tell them, "I saw your father walking your mother to the bus this morning/afternoon and they were holding hands."

One of my dear friends used to always tell me, "You're spoiled." She's absolutely right – I am spoiled – my husband spoils me lovely.

Another friend told me I was weird because my husband would come meet me for lunch everyday at my job after he retired. She always thought it was weird that we spent so much time together but then she would tell me she wanted what her parents had.

One day when we were on our way back to my job after lunch, a good friend stopped us and said, "I think it's beautiful that after all the years you've been together, every time I see you two you're always talking."

One of my husband's friends told me this right after I was introduced to him, "You know he's never going to marry you – right?" They talked for a bit and after he walked away I told my husband, "That's not your friend."

My husband's best friend new better. He always told me, "He's gonna marry you."

One of my friends asked me why we waited so long to get married and I answered, "If we knew the answer to that question, we probably would've got married sooner."

This is the **BIGGEST LIE** since creation began. You may have heard some people say, "I came into this world by myself and I'll leave by myself." Oh really? So no one carried you for 9 months? No one fertilized the embryo? You just appeared? You just grew up?

God new you needed someone before you did! You needed your mother to carry and bring you into this world, you needed your father to fertilize the embryo she carried before you were even conceived, and, more importantly, you needed God to create your mother and father in the first place – whether they were around or not.

Once you were born, you needed your family, friends, strangers, and teachers. Notice I didn't say education – I said teachers. When you are educated you have learned –

when you have learned you have been taught by teachers. We all know how teachers teach us in schools and we have all had someone in our past – an aunt, uncle, grandparent – that has given us words of wisdom, and we all know how life experiences can teach us lessons.

So now you're grown up and you're in love. Remember the first time you fell in love? Did you have any idea what love was or how to love someone? If you grew up in a loving, nurturing environment and your parents displayed genuine affection openly, you probably had a good idea. What if you didn't have that example? What if you grew up in an abusive environment? What if you saw your father beat your mother and vice/versa? If this was your only example, how good do you think your chances are of maintaining a relationship? What if you grew up in a loving, nurturing environment and your partner didn't? You want to get married? What if you are like one man I spoke with who told me, "All I remember about my mother is every time I turned around, there was a different man in her bed?" How do you think you would view women? What if you are like a young woman I spoke with you told me, "I came home from work early and caught my husband in bed with another woman – no man will ever hurt me again!" How do you think you would view men?

You need each other, you need constant, positive reinforcement, and you need everyone else and everything else around you.

In 'How Far Are You Willing To Go?' Jordan & Trenice were fortunate because they both came from loving families; however, Trenice didn't always have a loving & nurturing environment and it affected her relationship with Jordan. Her little sister Bunny was sad when Trenice got hurt and when Jordan apologized, Bunny screamed, "That's the same shit my Daddy said to me every time he hit my Mommy!"

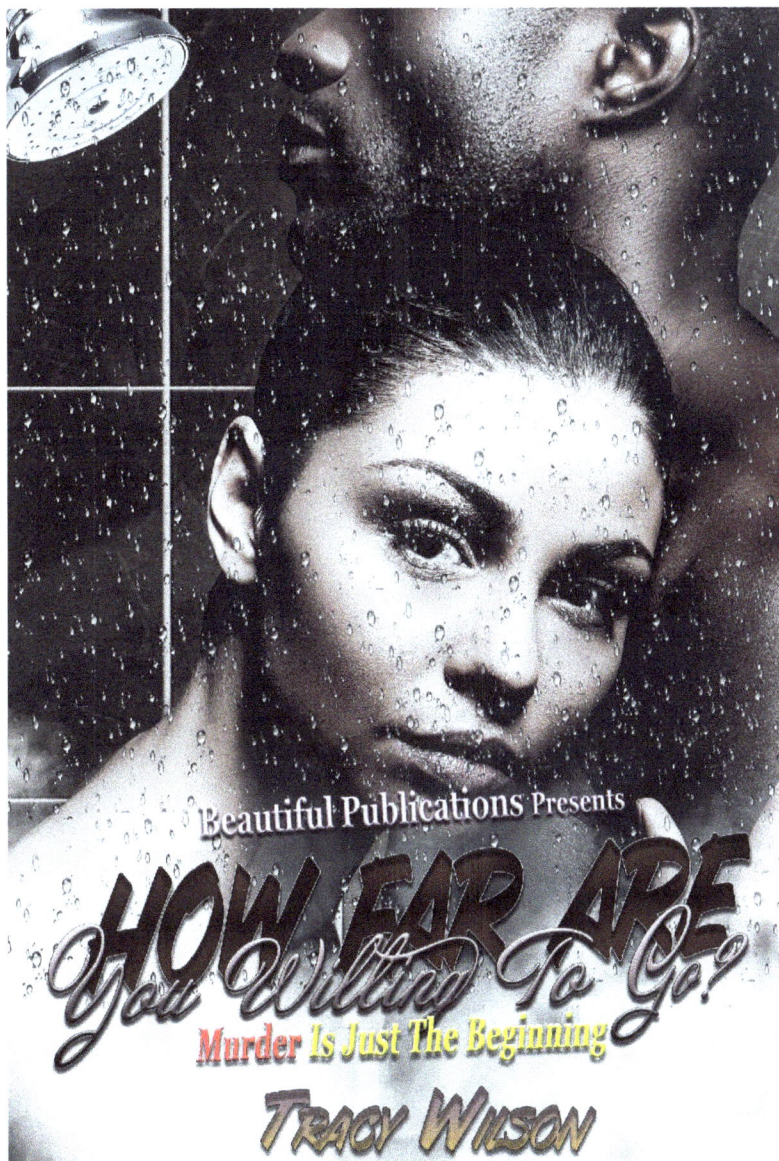

Beautiful Publications Presents

HOW FAR ARE You Willing To Go?

Murder Is Just The Beginning

TRACY WILSON

In the 'Twisted Series,' Bazil & Beautiee's childhood definitely had an affect on their relationship. Bazil had a great relationship with his parents and he was able to communicate with his father openly; however, Beautiee's relationship with her parents wasn't that great – especially when Beautiee was sent to live with her grandfather because her mother thought she was listening to them while they were having sex! Fortunately they both learned from their childhood and the best thing that happened with their children was that they saw their parents being affectionate, loving, and they also felt loved by them.

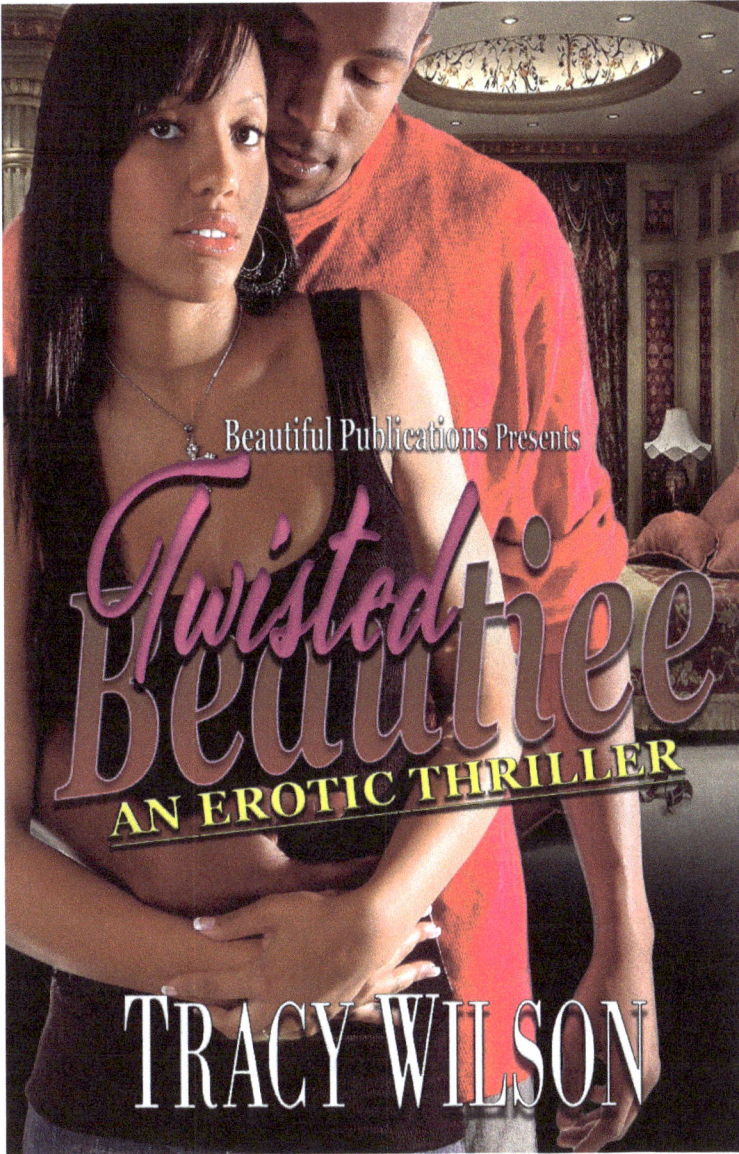

Beautiful Publications Presents

Twisted Beautiee

AN EROTIC THRILLER

TRACY WILSON

In 'My Christmas Miracle' the main character is the Baby that was surrounded by loving parents and loving grandparents from the moment she was conceived.

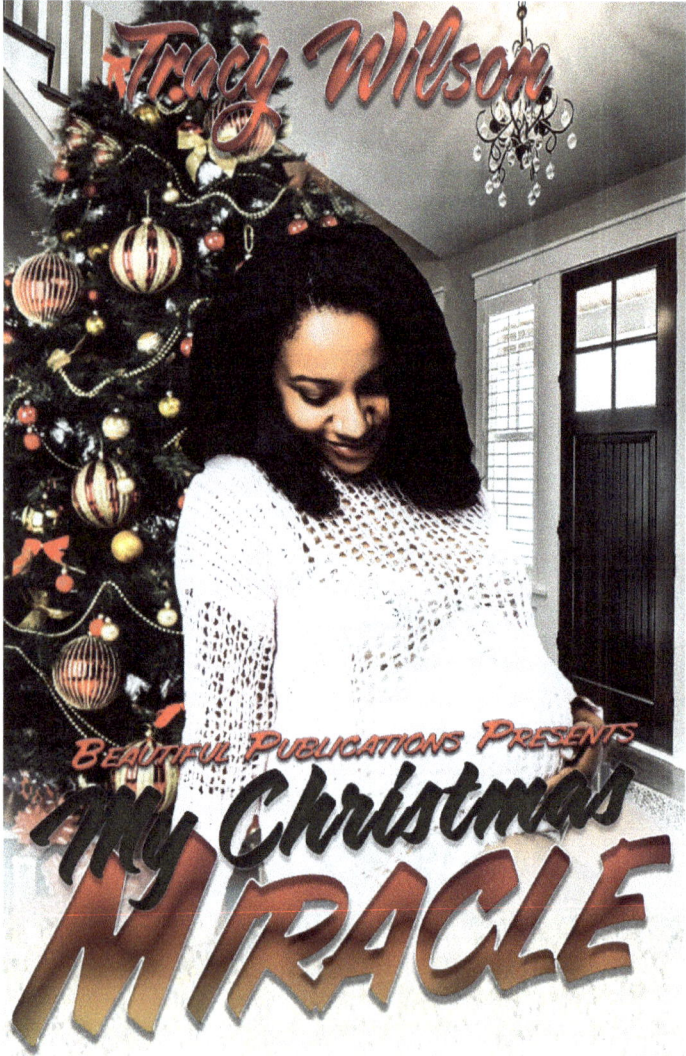

In 'Helen Vs Harmony,' the brothers were torn apart by their parents because one brother resented his father for leaving their mother and the other brother resented their mother for pushing their father away.

You and your partner turn and face each other, look in each other's eyes, and while you speak, your partner listens. This is important for the following reasons:

1. You need to say it.
2. You need to be sorry for it.
3. Your partner needs to hear it.
4. Your partner deserves an apology
5. Your partner needs to forgive you.

Now say aloud to your partner:

"When I told you I didn't need you I lied. I'm sorry for every time I ever said that to you and I will never say that to you again. Please forgive me. I love you. I need you. I thank God for you."

Now you and your partner turn and face each other, look in each other's eyes, and while your partner speaks, you listen.

Now give one another hugs, kisses, pounds, high fives, jump, and shout! You have just lifted a great weight off your shoulders and you have opened your minds to a new awareness! Welcome to the first day of the rest of your lives!

LISTENING IS AN ART – PART I

How many times have any of you said, "You don't listen to me!" Your partner is listening to you, but the problem may be that your partner isn't hearing what you are saying. Huh?

There are three learning styles:

Visual -   You learn best by what you
                   see, i.e., pictures, charts,
                   graphs, etc.

Auditory -   You learn best by what you
                   hear, i.e., tapes, lectures, etc.

Kinesthetic –   You need physical contact,
                   i.e., the 'hands on' approach.

I learned about the different learning styles after attending the 'Personal Power Weekend' with Anthony Robbins. The weekend included a listening exercise with 30 questions to help you understand how you listen and how you learn. If you have high scores in two or more sections, you have more than one strength.

After my husband and I completed the exercise, I wasn't surprised to find out that we were both Auditory Learners; however, we're also both Visual & Kinesthetic Learners with my husband being slightly more Visual while I'm slightly more Kinesthetic.

The following exercise will help you and your partner understand the different learning styles. Copy/type this link into your browser and it will give you a printable word document.

https://www.stetson.edu/administration/academic-success/media/Learning%20Style%20Questionnaire.docx

There are lots of choices online but I recommend the one above because it's easy to complete and it also has additional information to help you evaluate the questionnaire. After reading the evaluation I was really excited to learn that my husband and I are both multi-sensory learners!

You and your partner print out the Learning Style Questionnaire, fill it out, and compare your learning styles.

Are you balanced? Good! You and your partner communicate effectively. Is your learning style predominantly Auditory while your partner's is predominantly Visual? Great! <u>Your partner can learn to "hear" what you are saying and you can learn to "see" what your partner is saying</u>.

The Visual Learner: "You see what I'm saying?"

The Auditory Learner: "I heard that!"

The Kinesthetic Learner: "You feel me?"

Now that we've established how we learn, let's get back to listening. We need to <u>learn to listen</u> and we need to <u>learn how to listen</u>. The two go hand in hand.

LISTENING IS AN ART – PART II

One of the easiest ways to listen is to simply, "shut up!" If you are talking, you aren't listening. It's as simple as that. Remember when you were an infant and you had a pacifier? Remember when you had your own infants and you wanted them to be quiet? What did you do? You put the pacifier in their mouth!

Once when my husband and I were arguing I put a pacifier in my mouth. My husband looked at me strangely and asked, "Why are you sucking on a pacifier?" I took the pacifier out of my mouth and explained, "I'm not sucking on the pacifier. I'm letting you talk. I will listen to what you have to say and I won't say a word until you're finished. As long as this pacifier is in my mouth, I can't talk." Then I put the pacifier back in my mouth. He got the point.

How many times are you watching your favorite show and you start yelling because they don't see something, they don't hear something, or they're constantly interrupting each other because they're talking instead of listening?

This was definitely an issue in 'Caught In The Middle' because Lacey cheated on Darien instead of having a conversation with him and telling him how she was feeling.

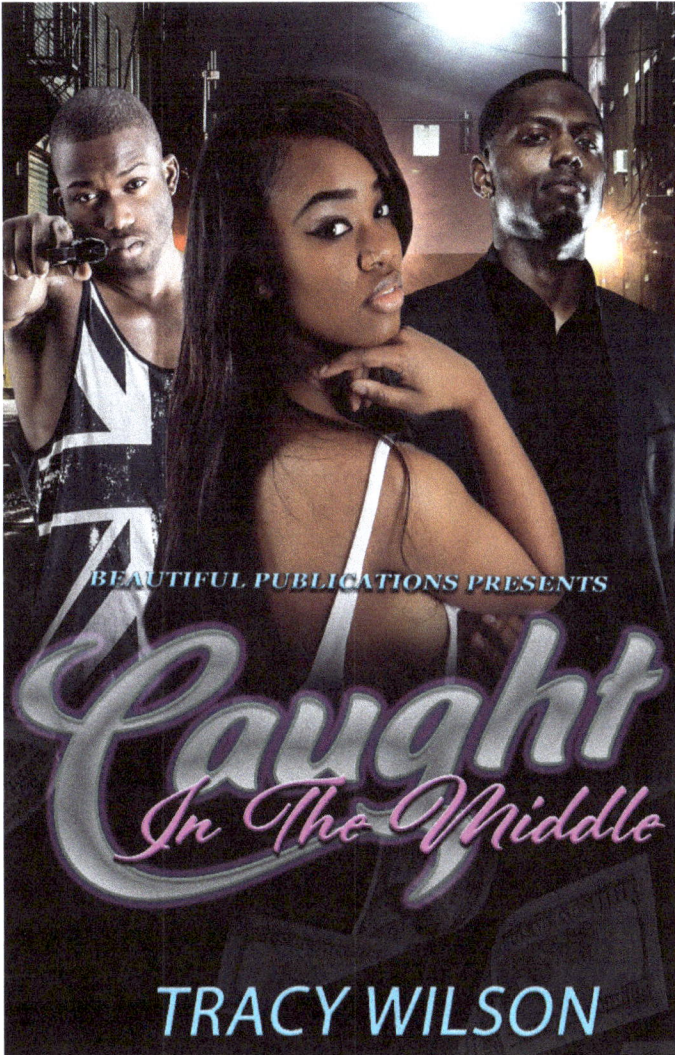

In 'Thirst Quencher' LaShonda lost her husband because she cheated on him instead of taking the time to have a conversation with him to let him know what her needs were.

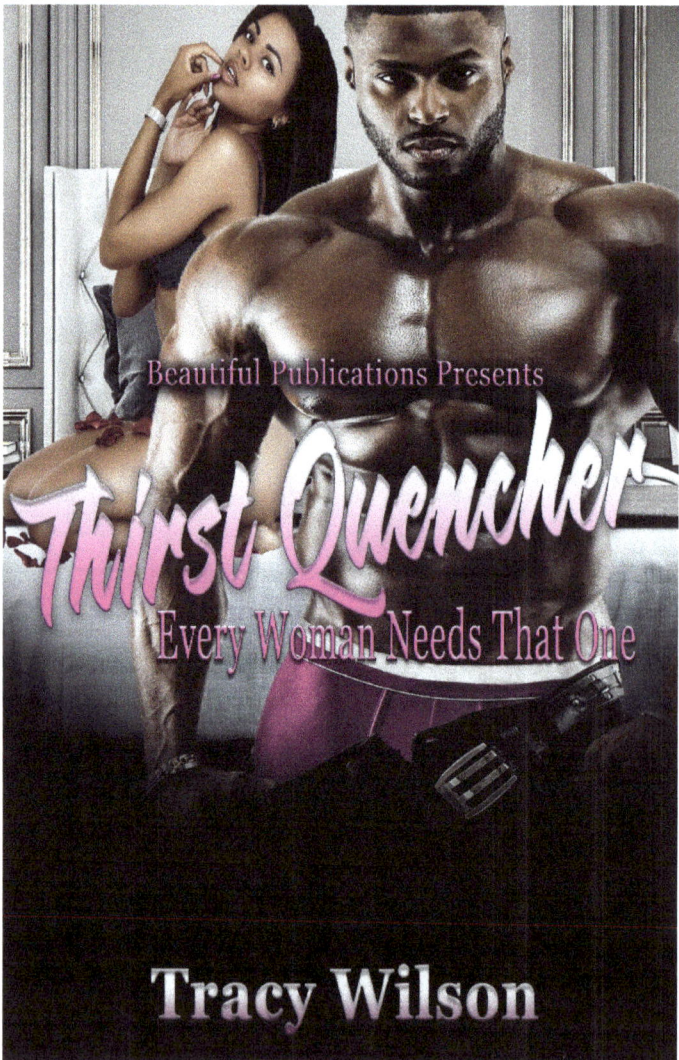

EXERCISE III

You and your partner think of a problem that you haven't been able to resolve because every time you try to resolve it, you begin to argue. One at a time, each of you take turns putting the pacifier in your mouth while listening to the other. It may seem silly at first, but do this a few times and you will both be in the habit of listening to one another. The end result will be that your arguments will be few and far between.

GENUINE AFFECTION

When it's just the two of you, you can cuddle, hold hands, and sit arm in arm, etc., yet, when you are out in public, you are embarrassed. Why? What is so embarrassing about genuine affection? How do you expect your children to know that you love each other and, more importantly, that you love them, if you don't display genuine affection with one another, and, more importantly, if you don't display it with them? If you stop and think right now about how you grew up, you know what I mean.

Did your mom and dad openly display their affection for one another? When you see the elderly holding hands/smooching does it bring back pleasant memories for you about your own parents/grandparents displaying genuine affection? Does it remind you of sitting in grandpa's lap and being held? If not, remember what we talked about in Chapter I? Think about that and think about your current relationship. Are you genuinely affectionate or does your partner have to ask for it? We all say, "I need a hug," sometimes – that's not what I mean.

While I was growing up, there were hugs, but I asked for most of them. To some this may not be a big deal, but you may not realize how important hugging is. I always make it a point to hug my husband, my children, my nieces/nephews, my grandparents/parents, and my friends/associates. Sure, they know I love them because I tell them, but the hug is a constant reinforcement of the love you have for them. It's fine to say, "I love you," but it's better to feel loved and to make others feel loved in return. Hugging isn't something that should be reserved for children or times of intimacy – hugging should be as normal and natural for you as the wave or the handshake. How can we expect our children to grow up feeling nurtured and loved if we don't give them genuine affection? How will they know how to be nurturing and loving in their relationships if we don't teach them by example?

EXERCISE IV

You and your partner give each other a hug and tell each other you love each other. Now hug your children and tell them you love them. The very next time you see your good friend/family member, give them a hug and tell them you love them. Remember how important it is to feel loved and make others feel loved in return. This is one of the most important exercises you can do in life for life.

We all want to be intimate and we all enjoy it. It feels good physically, psychologically, and emotionally, but according to medical experts, it's good for us too!

Kissing is the beginning of intimacy. Many of us remember how we would 'French Kiss' for hours on end. A serious tongue-tangling French Kiss exercises all the underlying muscles of the face – which could keep you looking younger and certainly looking happier. (Davis, Walton 1)

Kissing might even help you lose weight! During a really passionate kiss, you might burn two calories a minute – double your metabolic rate! (Stamford 1)

Kissing is an exciting excursion into the sensual. When you connect with someone you care about, it produces a sense of well-being and a kind of full bodied pleasure. It stops the buzz in your mind, quells anxiety, and heightens the experience of being present in the moment. It actually produces a lot of the physiological changes that meditation produces. (Davidson 1)

Sex drive and lust are triggered by testosterone in both men and women. Dopamine and norepinephrine kick in when romance begins. Oxytocin and vasopressin factor in at the attachment phase, bringing the sense of calm and peace you find with "the one." (Fisher 1) Oxytocin also lowers your blood pressure! Stimulation of the breasts, in both men and women, causes the brain to send a signal for the pituitary gland to release Oxytocin. (Turner 1)

Orgasm releases endorphins, the mind's natural mood relaxers and enhancers. (Gorkin 1) Semen contains hormones including testosterone, estrogen, prolactin, luteinizing hormones, and prostaglandins, and some of these are absorbed through the walls of the vagina and are known to elevate mood! (Kary 1)

Medical experts also believe sex can keep you young! One of the first longitudinal studies of aging began at Duke University in the '50s and reported in the December 1982 journal "Gerontologist" found that the frequency of sexual intercourse for men and the enjoyment of sex for women predicted longevity.
(Blum 1)

In a long-term study published in book form as Secrets of the Super Young, the key ingredients for looking younger are staying active and maintaining a good sex life. In a study of 3,500 people, ages 30 to 101, it was found that sex helps you look between four and seven years younger. (Weeks 1)

A more recent study, published in the January 1990 issue of the Archives of Internal Medicine, reported that nearly 74% of married men over 60 remain sexually active, as do 56% of married women. And an April 1988 study on Sexual Interest and Behavior in Healthy 80 to 102 year olds published in the Archives of Sexual Behavior found that 63% of men and 30% of women are still having sexual intercourse. Given that by the age of 80 or older there are 39 men for every 100 women, lack of opportunity may well account for a large portion of such gender differences.
(Meston 1)

The best way to maintain sexuality in later years is to never stop making love. (Love 1)

EXTRA-CURRICULAR ACTIVITIES

Personally, I believe that your extra-curricular activities shouldn't include inviting other people between you and your partner. If you and your partner attend sex conventions, orgies, sex clubs, etc., and you and your partner watch what's going on around you and then jump each other – in other words, you are only into each other - then that's fine because it's kept between the two of you – but it's something else when you invite other people between you.

First of all, intimacy is no longer there. Once you share yourself with someone other than your partner, the intimacy is gone. Secondly, your partner will easily develop feelings for someone else and vice/versa. In my opinion, if this is okay with you and your partner, why bother becoming a couple or getting married? Every time you and your partner share yourselves with someone else, you make a mockery of your commitment to one another. I'm not saying don't play. I'm just saying don't play with anyone else but each other. Some fantasies are better left as just that. You may not agree with this but, in my opinion, the best way to stay intimate with one another is to keep it between the two of you. Like my husband said, "You never want another man to know what your woman feels like." It's yours and yours alone – cherish it.

In the 'Twisted Series,' a threesome went from a threesome, to a foursome, to two gruesome murders that led to Beautiee being arrested for two counts of murder and the attempted murder of her husband!

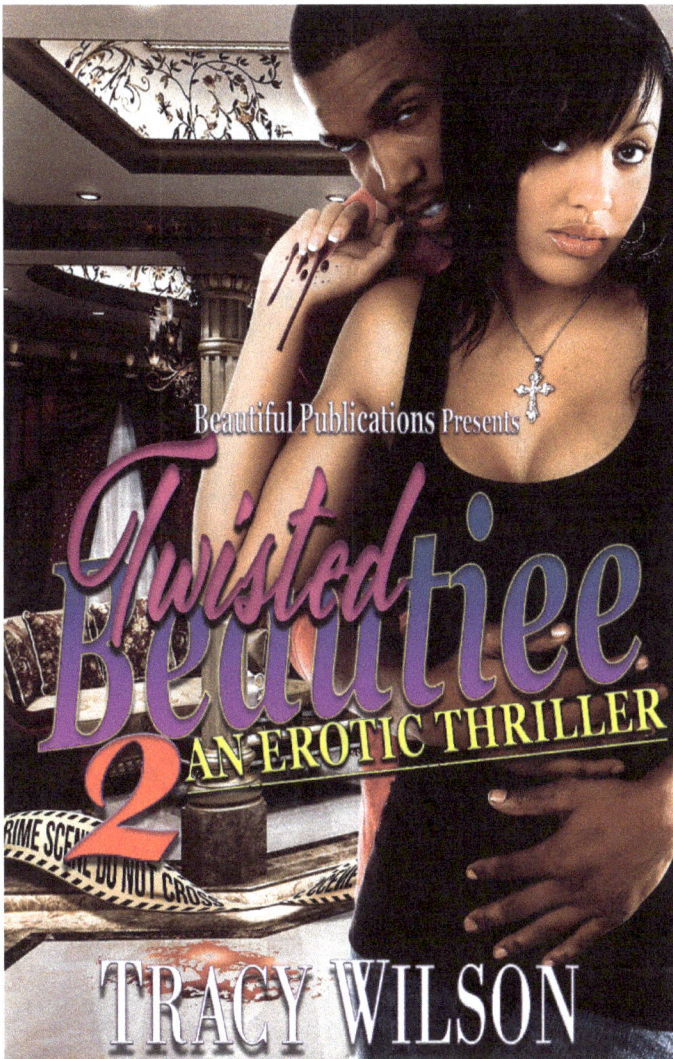

In 'Obsidian Heart,' Jade was determined to fight for her marriage and when she found Amber in her husband's conference room things took a psychotic turn for the worse.

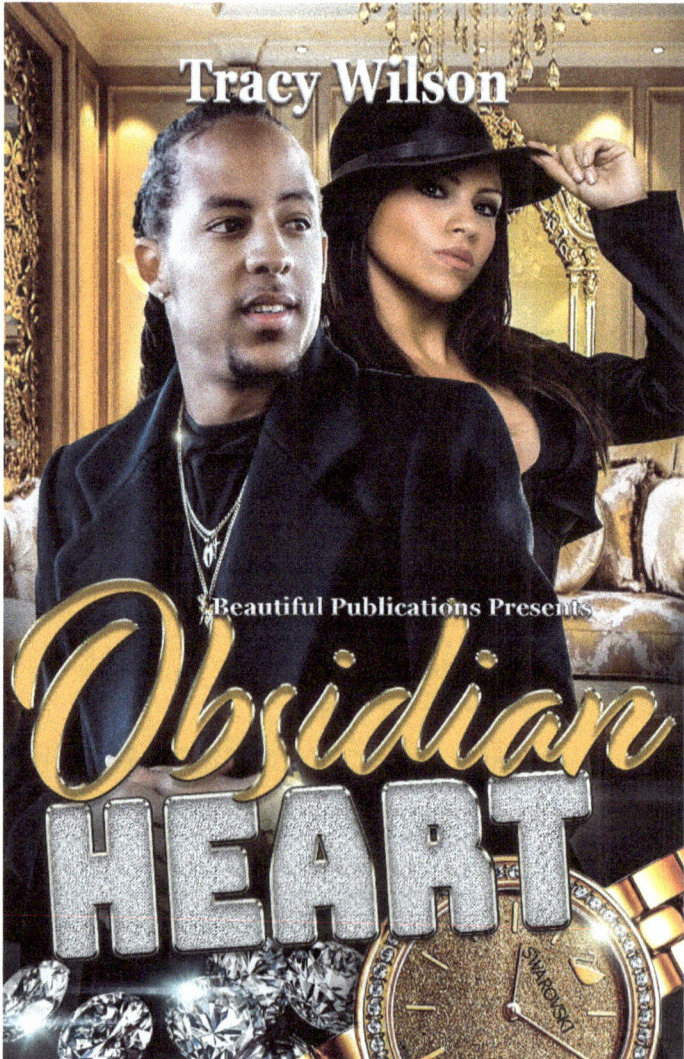

In 'Russian Roulette,' John & Susan had no idea what they were walking into when they accepted Gary & Brenda's invitation.

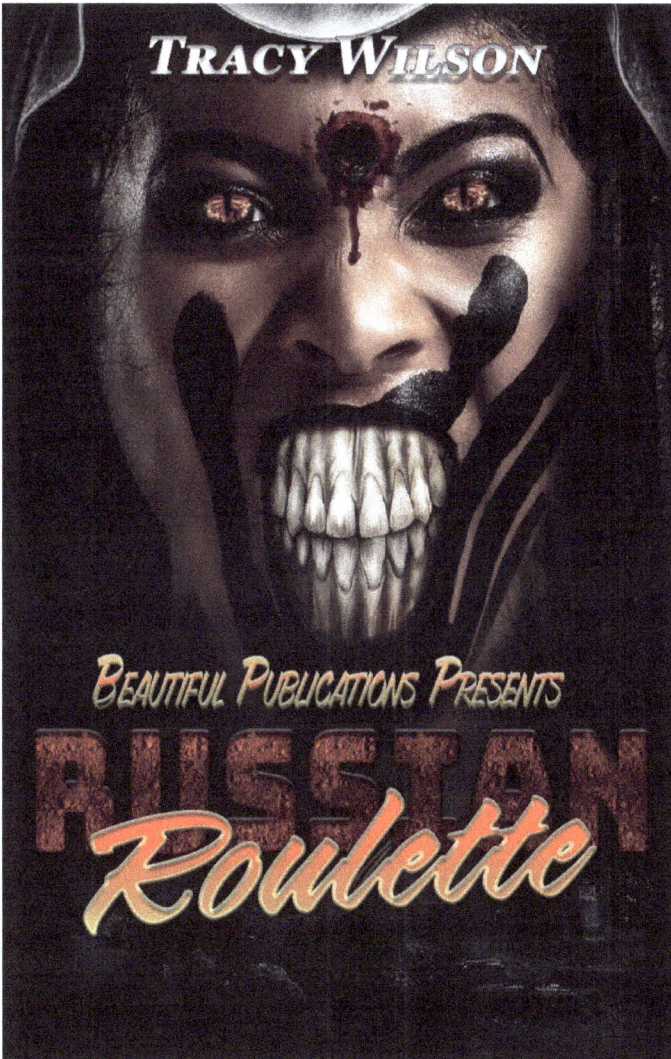

DO IT EVERYWHERE!

One of my male associates gave me this advice when he found out I was writing this book, "Make sure you put this in your book – do it everywhere! Me and my girl have done it at the drive in theatre; we've done it outside…" This started a conversation where other people just volunteered places they've done it; At the movies, in the park, up on the roof, up against the wall of a building in an alley, outside in the rain, in the back seat of the car, in an elevator (if you're into voyeurism, this is perfect because the security people that work the cameras also watch what's going on in the elevators). One of my friends told me, "Me and my man went outside in the snow, took off all our clothes, did it in the snow, then got dressed and went back inside – the combination of the heat from our bodies and the cold from the snow was such a turn on!"

Go 'head with your bad selves!   We'll live vicariously through y'all 'cause I'm not doing it everywhere; however, in 'How Far Are You Willing To Go?' when Trenice had her 'Bridal Shower,' nobody bothered getting a room and when Jordan & Trenice visited the club, 'Just Ask,' they did it out in the open!

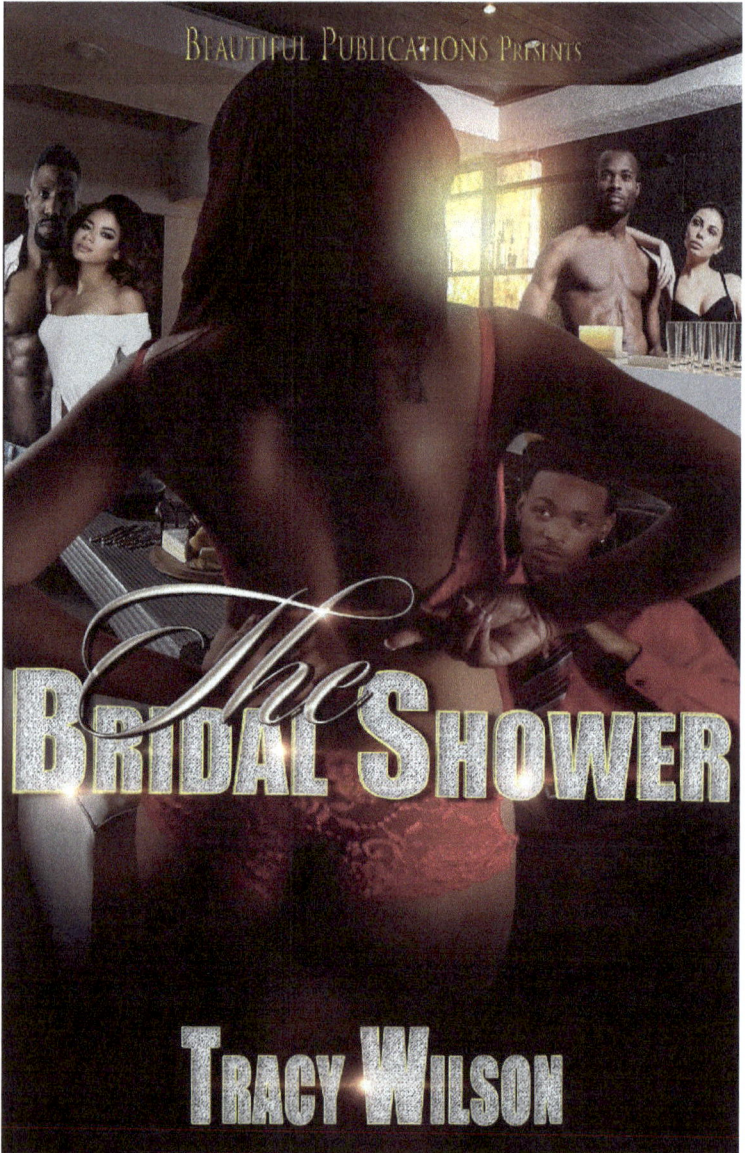

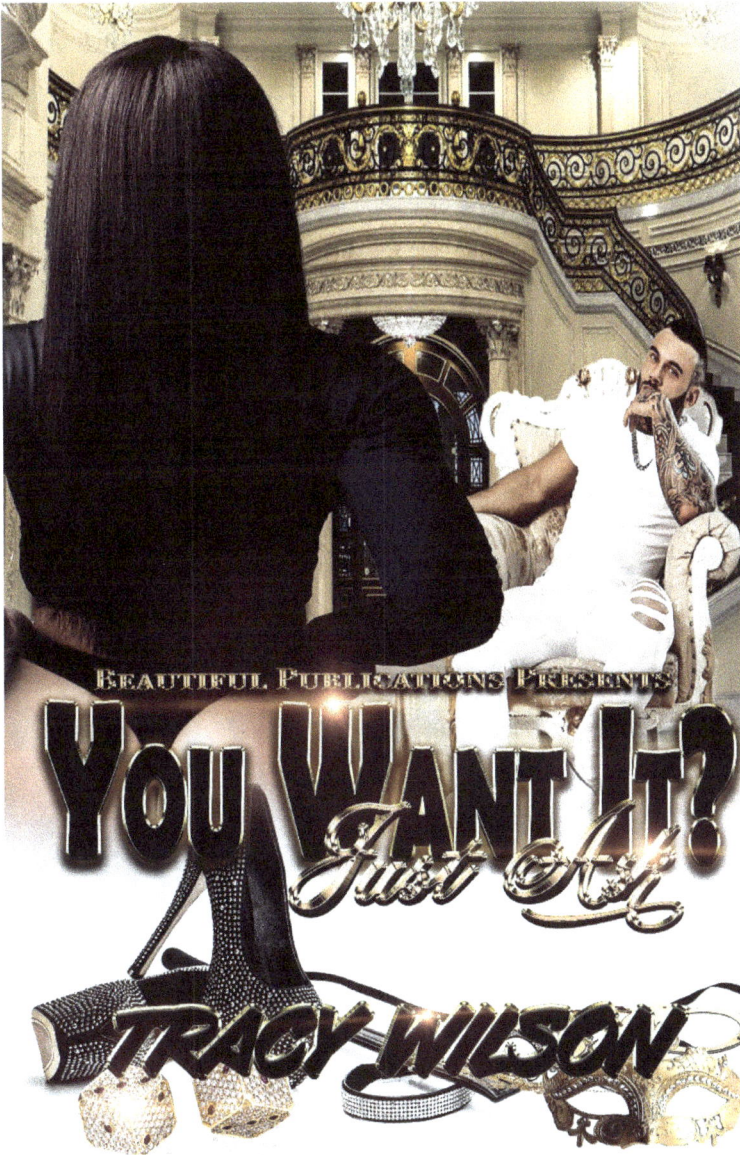

In the 'Twisted Series,' Bazil & Beautiee did it in the Judge's Chambers!

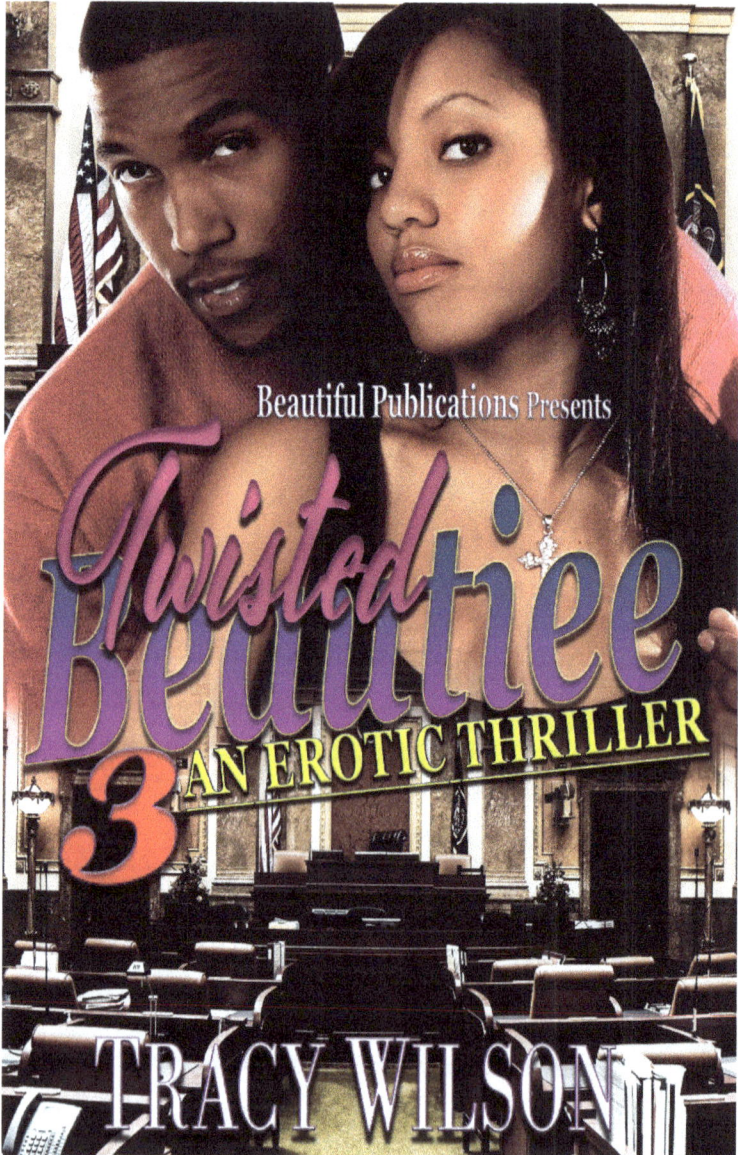

Chandler & Starr did it on their patio and when they knew their neighbors could hear them, it turned them on!

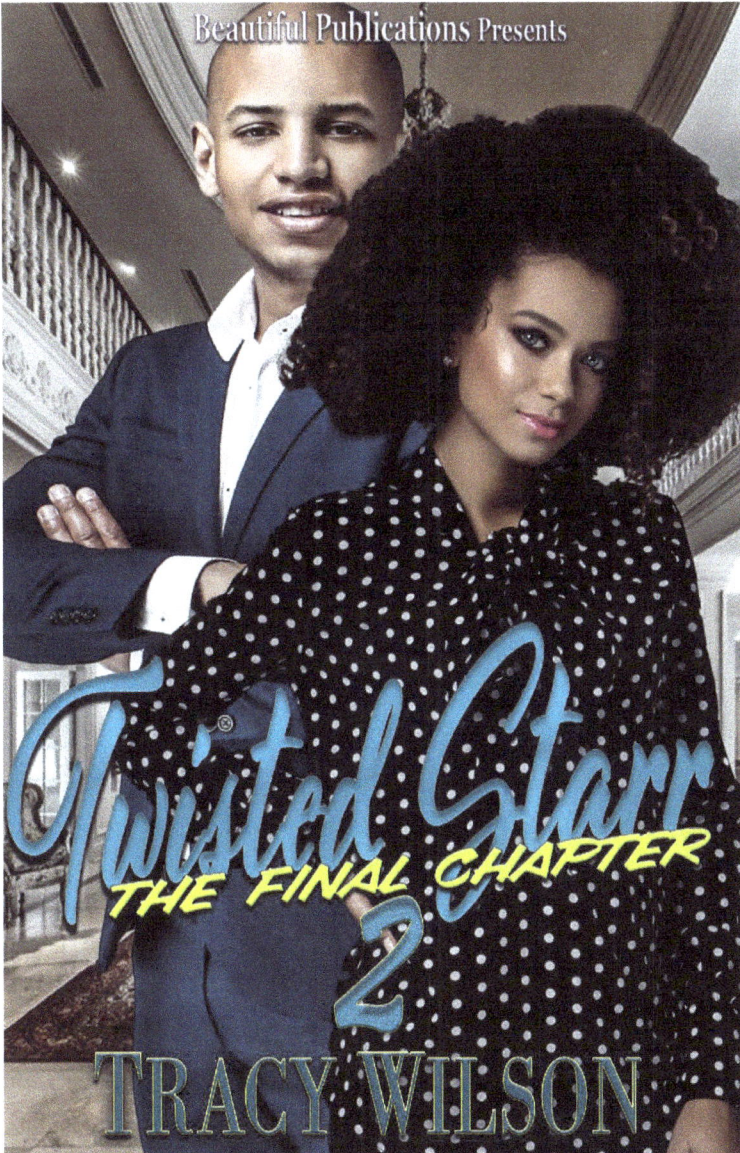

As soon as Mary found the nude beach, she couldn't wait for Wayne to do it in the water!

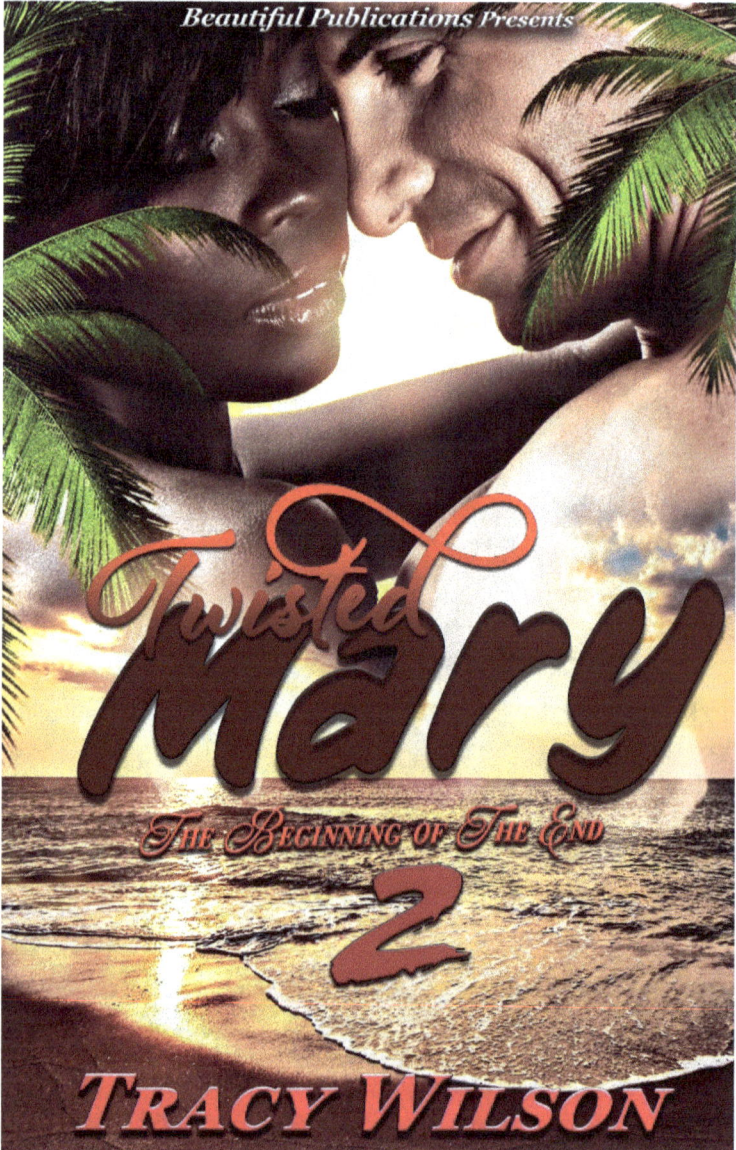

It was a 'Twisted Christmas' for all the parents after the children received their gifts – Bazil, Beautiee, Troy, & Keisha did it in the same hotel; Charles & Theresa did it in their bedroom, Chandler & Starr did it in their bedroom, and Wayne & Mary did it in Chandler & Starr's guest room!

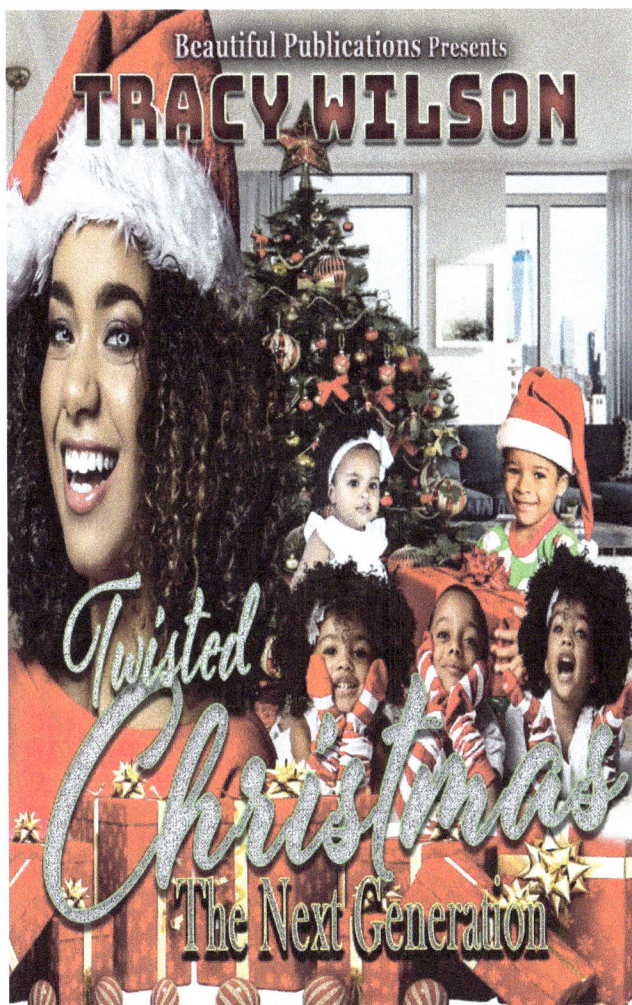

In 'Yes Please,' my characters did it on the kitchen table filled with food!

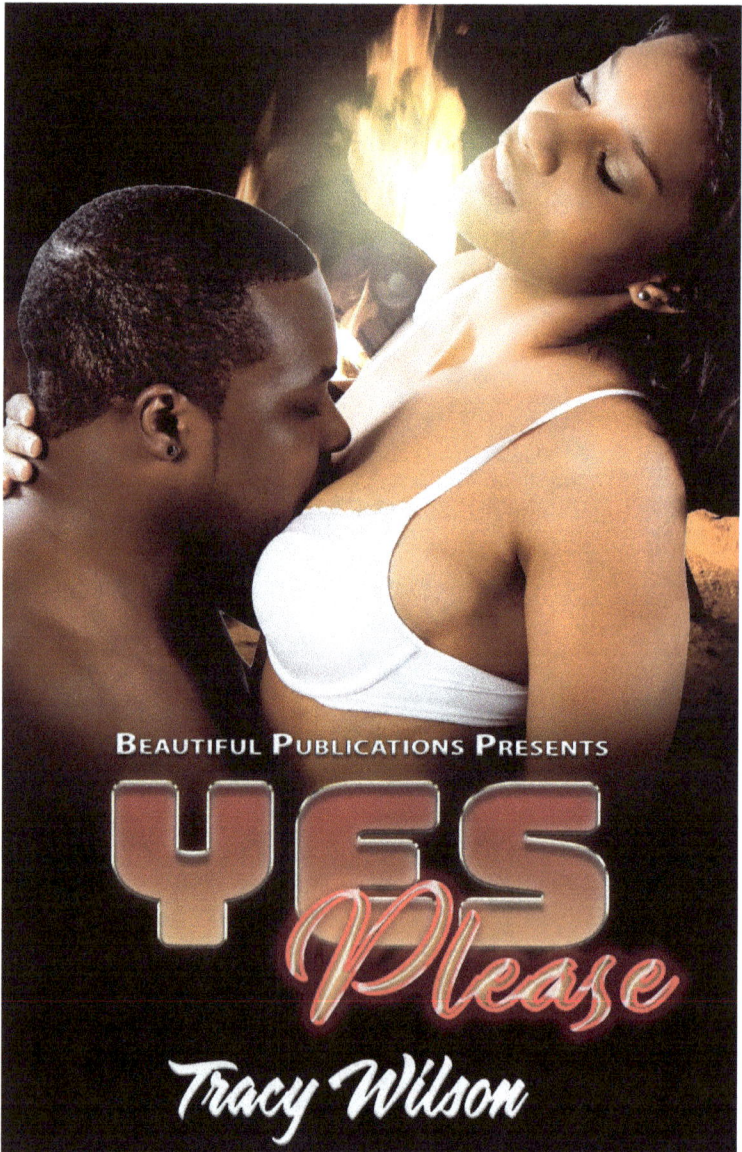

In 'Erotic Zombies,' the zombies did it in cemeteries, parks, backyards, and other public places - but I know for a fact that zombies aren't the only ones doing this. Have you ever done it in a cemetery?

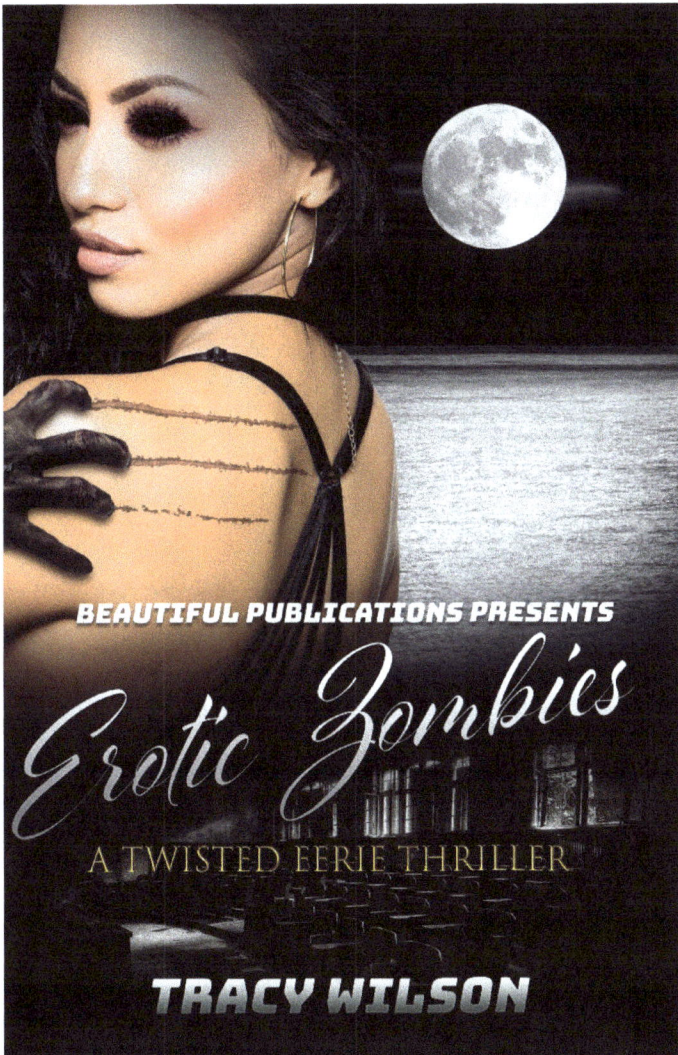

BEAUTIFUL PUBLICATIONS PRESENTS

Erotic Zombies

A TWISTED EERIE THRILLER

TRACY WILSON

In 'His Best Friend,' Clarisse caught Rashad servicing one of his clients in the shower at the gym!

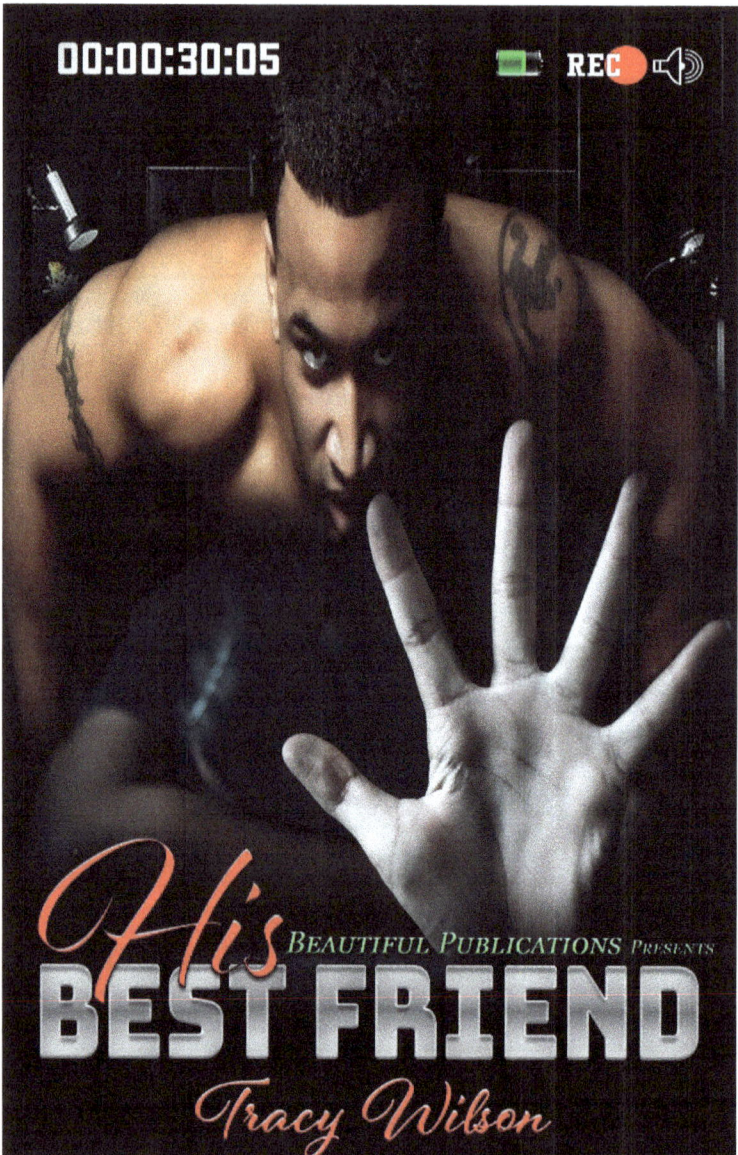

In 'The Ultimate Con,' Flick & Snow did it in the hotel at the Mohegan Sun Casino.

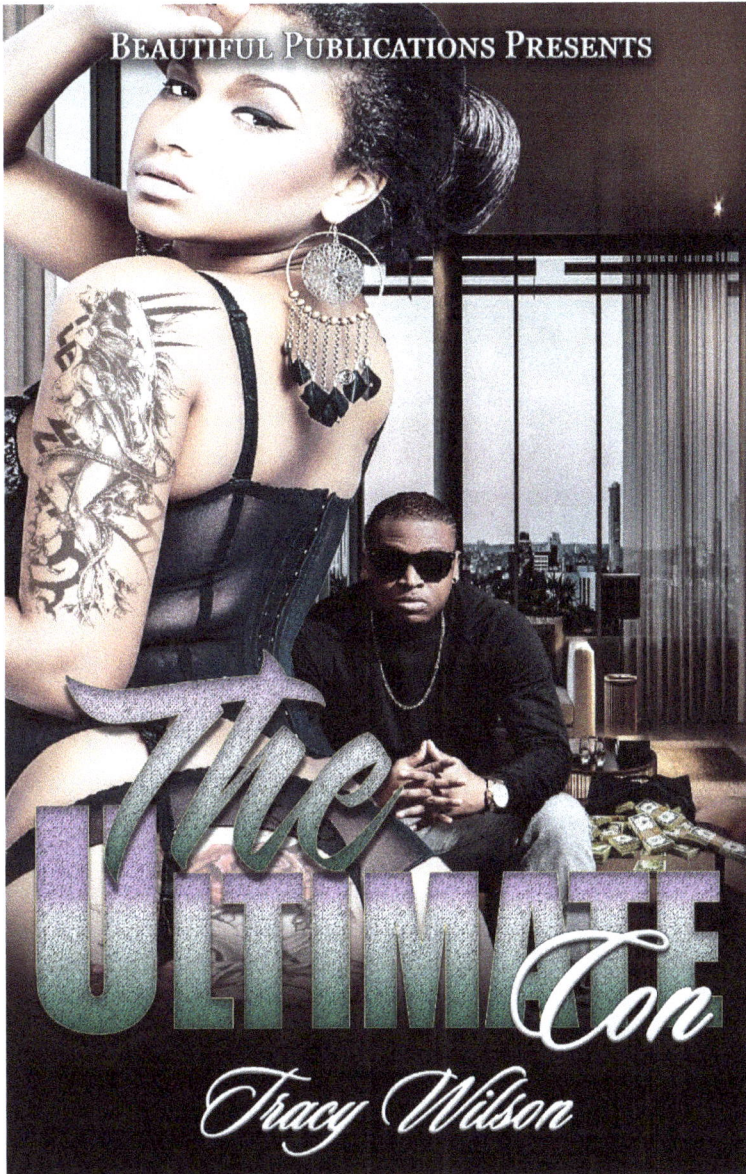

In 'Stalked By Magic,' Jake & Kevin took a trip to Heaven & Hell in the stall in the Men's room at the club!

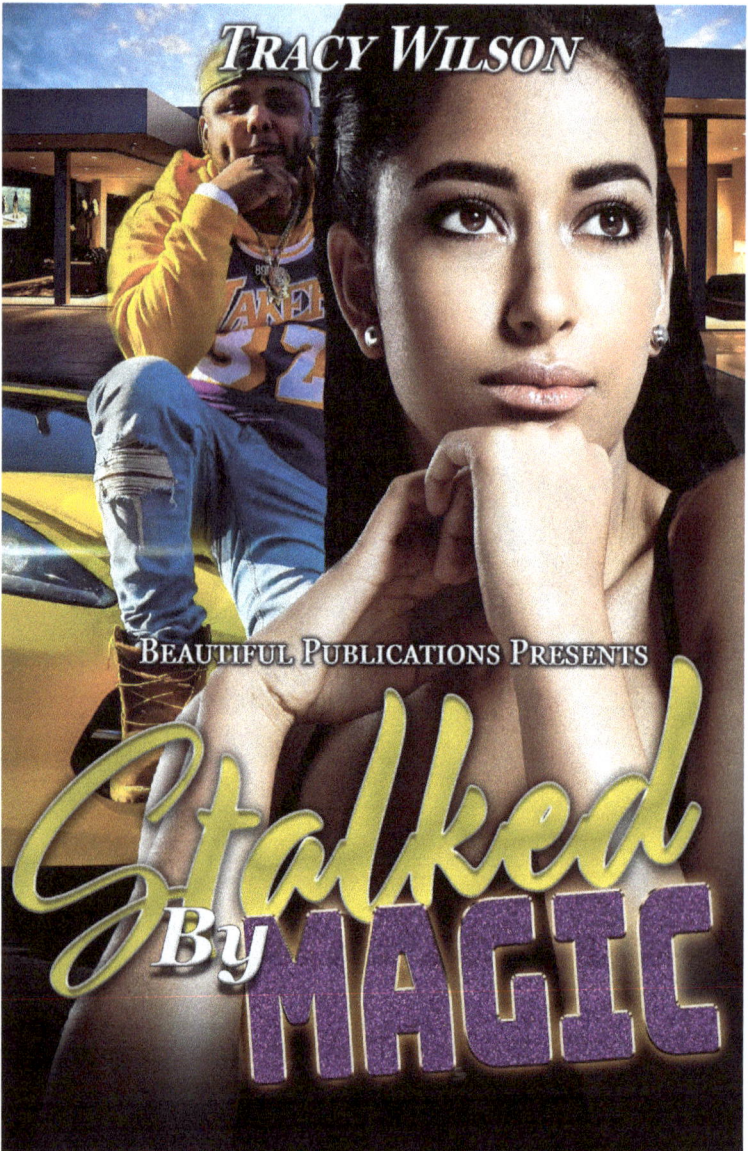

In 'Happy New Year,' Darnell & Chelle did it on the balcony and it didn't bother them that other couples could watch – in fact, Chelle handed someone her phone to record and take pictures!

EXERCISE V

You and your partner go be intimate!

I did my own survey to find out who, the what, and the why of oral sex. My findings are as follows:

83% of those who answered my survey were male, 17% were female. This is great – particularly because when asked, "Do you perform oral sex on your partner," 100% answered yes! When asked, "Why? Is it for your partner, yourself, or both of you," 66% answered for both of us. When asked, "Is there something you would like your partner to do that they're not doing," 66% answered no, 18% answered my partner does what he should, and 16% answered push my head harder. When asked, "Does your partner perform oral sex on you," 57% answered yes! When asked, "Do you like it," 71% answered yes! When asked, "Do you feel your partner is good at performing oral sex" 83% answered hell yea, and 17% answered yes! When asked, "On a scale of 1 to 10, how would you rate your partner's overall performance of oral sex," 50% answered 10, 33% answered 8, and 17% answered don't even go there! One of my girlfriends told me, "Oh I give myself at least an 8! When asked, "Do you 'cum' in your partner's mouth and vice/versa," 71% answered yes! When asked, "Does your partner swallow your 'cum' and vice/versa, 99% answered yes! 33% of those who answered my survey were between the ages of 21 and 25, 16% were between the ages of 26 and 30, 33% were between the ages of 31 and 40, and 16% were aged 50 and above.

In addition to my findings, some researchers report that 80% of single men and women between the ages of 25 and 34 and 90% of those married and under 25 years of age have participated in oral sex. (Bullough 1)

There is an increasing frequency of the practice among adolescents – they recognize it as a means of sex without fear of pregnancy. Heterosexual couples use it for the same reason. Partners may use it as a means of expressing deep intimate feelings, or it may be incorporated in foreplay or afterglow when other techniques are used to achieve orgasm, or it can be the only means of reaching an orgasm. Oral sex is also used when a male has difficulty attaining an erection or if intercourse is painful. It has also been used by people with disabilities, such as spinal cord injuries, or during late pregnancy or after child-birth when intercourse can be dangerous or painful. (Bullough 2)

This topic is one of the biggest issues in a relationship. In fact, in some relationships, oral sex can be more of an issue than sexual intercourse. I will give you my personal opinions about oral sex, as well as opinions from others that I have spoken with. Please note: there is no right or wrong when it comes to oral sex. If you don't agree with something you read in the next few pages, that doesn't make it wrong – it just means we agree to disagree. Whether or not you engage in oral sex, everyone can benefit from this chapter.

For men, it seems that performing oral sex on their partner is something they enjoy. Most men I've talked to enjoy giving their partner pleasure. There are some men who enjoy performing oral sex on their partner even though their partner may not necessarily like it, simply because they enjoy it.

Besides the obvious (proper hygiene) most men feel that oral sex is something that should occur with that "special someone" because of the risk of STDs. I was happy to learn this particular fact because it shows that men take this just as seriously as women do and that, contrary to popular belief, they don't just do it to "anyone and everyone."

Naturally, men want their partners to perform oral sex on them as well. When a man meets a woman that isn't into oral sex, this causes a problem because, simply put, "some men can't do without it." Some men I've spoken with feel that if they don't "get it at home" they will "get it elsewhere." I personally don't agree with this and I'm not telling you that you should do it, but you need to know the truth and there it is. A friend of mine gave this advice to a woman, "You should do it – you'll keep your man home!" Thankfully, there are some men who feel that if their partner doesn't like it or isn't willing to do it, then they will stay with their partner and do without it. My advice is this: if oral sex is that important to you, establish that fact early on and if your partner isn't willing to do it, that's the time to decide if you are willing to stay in the relationship. Furthermore, and this is for men as well as women, don't make a promise you don't intend to keep. Men, don't promise to love, honor, and forsake all others when you know damn well you're going somewhere else because she won't do it. Ladies, don't tell him, "I'll do it when we get married," if you don't mean it. First of all, if you're gonna do it, you're gonna do it. Secondly, if you think once you get married you can say, "I'm not doing that," and there won't be a problem, you're dead wrong!

Ladies, if you're doing it, do it because you enjoy it too. Men can sense when you're just going through the motions because you think he likes that and if he cares anything about you, he won't want it that way. If you want to know if you're doing it right, ask him! Believe me, he'll let you know how you're doing – and if you need more practice, he'll be more than happy to oblige! If ever there was a case for "practice makes perfect" sucking dick is it!

SHE WANTS TO SUCK YOUR DICK!

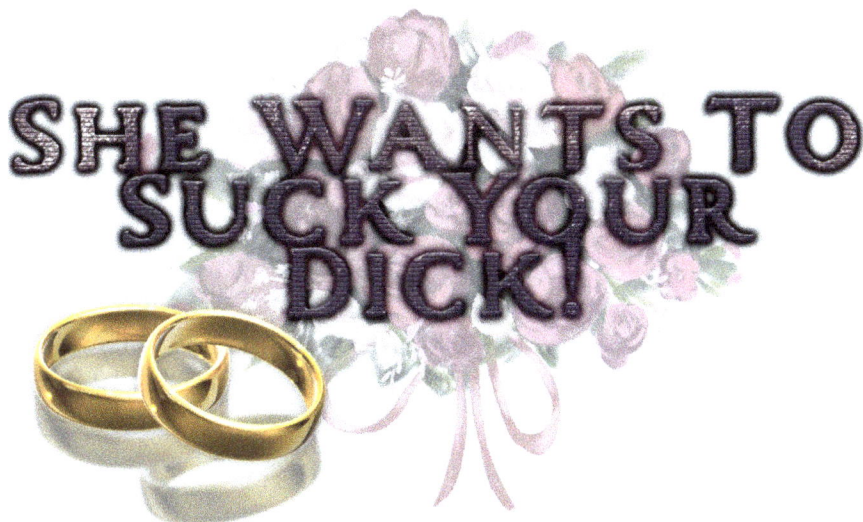

If she's not doing it, she's thinking about doing it. But you need to know what she's thinking and why.

1. First of all, if there was any type of trauma (rape, incest) you have to be patient! If you don't care enough about women in general to understand how trauma can affect intimacy, don't even bother with her. Thankfully, most men are very sensitive to a woman's needs and, if anything they want to help her through it or at least, wish they had been told about it. Many women are afraid to talk about it because they don't want you to think less of them and they don't want anyone to know – especially you – because they are so ashamed.

2. Believe it or not, there are actually some men that don't want their partner to perform oral sex on them! Some men feel the woman is a whore if she wants to do it, and some women want to do it but they know their partner will think of them as a whore so they don't even bring it up. I spoke with one man who said, "I would never ask someone I care about to do that – I feel I would be degrading her – I'd rather pay a whore to do it." I also spoke with a woman who asked her man to let her do that and he told her, "No – only whores do that." I don't know about you, but if you think I'm a whore, I wouldn't even want to stay with you – let alone suck your dick!

3. Well I was raised...

    One of my girlfriends is a regular bus passenger. She has heard many conversations on the bus, so she approached me one day and said, "I've heard your conversations and I personally don't think there's anything wrong with your discussions, but I'm a virgin and I believe you should wait until you're married." Some women also feel that no matter how much they want to do it, they shouldn't simply because it's wrong. I can't tell anyone how to live his or her life. You have to decide for yourself what your values should be and what's right for you.

4. I want to but every time I get into it, he grabs my head and I start gagging because he pushes my head down to hard!

We know it feels good and you enjoy it but you have to learn to control yourself! If your partner is choking, that's not fun for either of you because your partner will stop what they're doing and may even get angry. As much as you enjoy it, you have to remember – your partner does too, so why take that away from them? If you control yourself just a little – you can grab your partner's head, but let your partner determine how far your dick goes in their mouth – it will be a win-win for both of you! Trust me on this – if you let your partner have control you may start getting some deep throat action! The more relaxed your partner is, the further your dick will go in their mouth – believe me!

5. What if he comes in my mouth? He wants me to swallow his 'cum' – is it safe?

   a. Some men know that this is a problem and they don't care. Well, for those of you that don't care, you should. Trust has to be a major factor when it comes to oral sex. Thankfully, most men are not so selfish that they won't consider this – in fact, if you tell them you don't want them to 'cum' in your mouth, they won't.

b. For those of you who are worried about swallowing his 'cum,' don't be. According to medical experts, it's perfectly safe to swallow semen.

No one becomes sick from swallowing semen, and so there is no such thing as too much. (Klien 1)

If you're in a monogamous (single-partner) relationship, have both tested HIV negative for a sufficiently long period for the virus to have shown up, and neither of you has been diagnosed with another STD, it's
relatively safe to swallow semen. (Levine 1)

Healthy semen is safe to swallow, and it contains only about 5 calories per ejaculation. (Bullough 3)

In 'My Christmas Miracle,' the Baby will have you laughing your ass off as she tells you what she thinks and how she feels about swallowing semen:

"I laughed to myself as I thought about how conversations would go if our parents only knew how we interacted with each other before we reached our destination. They had no idea how boring it was inside our father's balls or how confused we were when we were shot down the throat instead of being shot into the vagina. Whenever sperm was shot down the throat we were really confused – imagine going straight down to the bottom of an acid volcano, only to be burned alive before they knew what was happening – or better yet – being spit into a cloth or a toilet! If I had a choice, I'd rather feed Mommy – at least I'd be serving a purpose before I die, unless Mommy's allergic to semen. Personally, I believe that no one is really allergic to semen because if that's the case, the same thing would happen to the vagina. I think what's really happening is that the sperm realize they're not where they're supposed to be and those symptoms described are actually the sperm having tantrums as children due when they're angry – LOL!"

6.   He Talks Too Damn Much!

A woman once told me, "I couldn't suck my husband's dick if I wanted to – he told all his friends I won't suck his dick so now, if I do, he will probably tell all his friends – oh, my wife sucks my dick now – and I don't want everyone in my business." Do I need to elaborate?

EXERCISE VI

You and your partner go have oral sex!

AFTERGLOW

We all like a nice warm, cozy fireplace right? The log is burning, a nice warmth is coming from the fire place, and you snuggle down with a good book, nice music, a glass of wine, or whatever you choose, with whomever you choose. It's so peaceful you can hear the wood crackling in the fireplace – maybe you can even hear the crickets outside or the wind whistling, and you snuggle down even more, feeling totally relaxed, totally calm. You've completely let go of all the stresses of the day and when you realize the fire's about to go out, without thinking about it, subconsciously, automatically, you put another log on the fire to keep it burning. Well, relationships require the exact same effort!

It's so easy for us all to keep the fire burning in the fireplace and in the bedroom, but we tend to forget the fire in our relationships. Some of you are thinking, "Well, if

I'm keeping the fire burning in the bedroom, then what's the problem?" There isn't a problem if you're just in the relationship for sex. But most relationships are more than that and most of us want it all.

Now we don't all have fireplaces so we can't all run out and buy logs and for those of us that do have fireplaces, you can't burn logs 24-7. But in Chapters I, II, & III, we learned how much we need each other, how communication and listening go hand in hand, and how important genuine affection is. In my opinion, those chapters are the foundation of all relationships – you can't have an afterglow if you haven't started the fire in the first place. But once you get the fire going right, you can keep the afterglow going for a lifetime.

When your partner comes home from work and vice/versa, most of you probably give them a hug/kiss and ask, "How was your day?" No big deal right? Wrong! The mere fact that you are asking the question is letting your partner know immediately – I'm here. I care. One of my friends told me, "Before I got divorced, my husband and I were in the house for 2 months and we didn't say one word to each other."

So your partner is home, you cook dinner, and before you sit down to eat with your family, you notice the candles. A smile comes across your face and you begin to reminisce about the last candlelight dinner you had. You remember how, just like with the fireplace, it was so peaceful, you were so calm, it was so romantic… then, as if you've been programmed, you tell yourself, "Oh these are for special occasions," and you put the candles away. But you just got finished reading my book. You want to keep the fire burning in your relationship. You love the afterglow. You realize that every day can be a special occasion. You change your mind – you bring out those candles and you light them! Your family watches as you light the candles and they ask, "What's the occasion? What are we celebrating?" "I just want to have dinner by candlelight," you tell them as you light the last candle. Instantly, everyone relaxes and enjoys their meal. You and your partner glance across the table at each other and you both smile as you realize you are right back in that moment where it was so peaceful, so calm, so romantic… then you are jarred back into reality – the phone rings, someone's at the door, the kids are screaming… and you jump up to handle the situation, clear the table, wash the dishes, etc., and when you're done, you look and see those candles are still burning. When you walk down the street and you see another couple holding hands, if you are with your partner, you will grab their hand or if not, you will instantly recall the last time you held hands and how good it felt. Or, perhaps you'll walk by another couple kissing each other and you will instantly recall the last time you kissed your partner and a smile will come across your face as you remember how loved you felt. You'll walk further and you'll see two friends that haven't seen each other in a long time hugging each other and you'll instantly recall the last time you saw your best friend. If it's been a while and you miss them, you remind yourself to give them a call and tell them you miss them, you were thinking about them, and you want to get together. You'll walk some more and you'll see a mother/father hugging their child and you'll instantly recall hugging/kissing your own children, nurturing them, and a smile comes across your face as you realize how much you love them and, more importantly, how much they know it.

It starts to rain and as you put up your umbrella, you instantly recall the last time you and your partner walked in the rain together, or perhaps you recall making love while listening to the rain hit your windows. A big smile comes across your face and you begin to feel flushed as you can almost feel the orgasm you had then… you hope it rains all day and if it stops raining, you hope it starts raining again when your partner gets home.

When you get to your office you turn on your computer and as you look at your favorite screensaver you instantly recall your last family vacation, or you begin to look forward to your coming vacation. You imagine walking along the beach or in the moonlight with your partner, getting away from it all, and you look at the calendar and start counting the days.

Perhaps your screensaver is your wedding picture and every time you see it you instantly recall your wedding day, your vows, and your commitment to each other day after day, month after month, year after year, and as you continue to look at this screensaver you realize the children are grown up and have their own lives, and it's just the two of you and a smile comes across your face as you look forward to the future.

And then, someone comes by your desk and says, "Good morning – how are you today?" and they just look at you and they already know the answer.

EXERCISE VII

You and your partner sit down with a pad & pencil. Write a letter as if someone asked the question, "What's your partner like?" Describe in detail how good your partner makes you feel, how considerate they are, how they're always there for you when you need them, etc. Use specific examples as you reminisce on how you first met, what your partner does to cheer you up when you're down, what you feel your partner's strengths are, what you're favorite activities with your partner are, the best part of your lovemaking, etc. When you're done, you and your partner exchange letters.

In my coffee series, the 'Coffee Complement' is a journal you can both carry with you so when you're feeling nostalgic throughout the day, you don't have to wait until you get home to write down your thoughts and feelings.

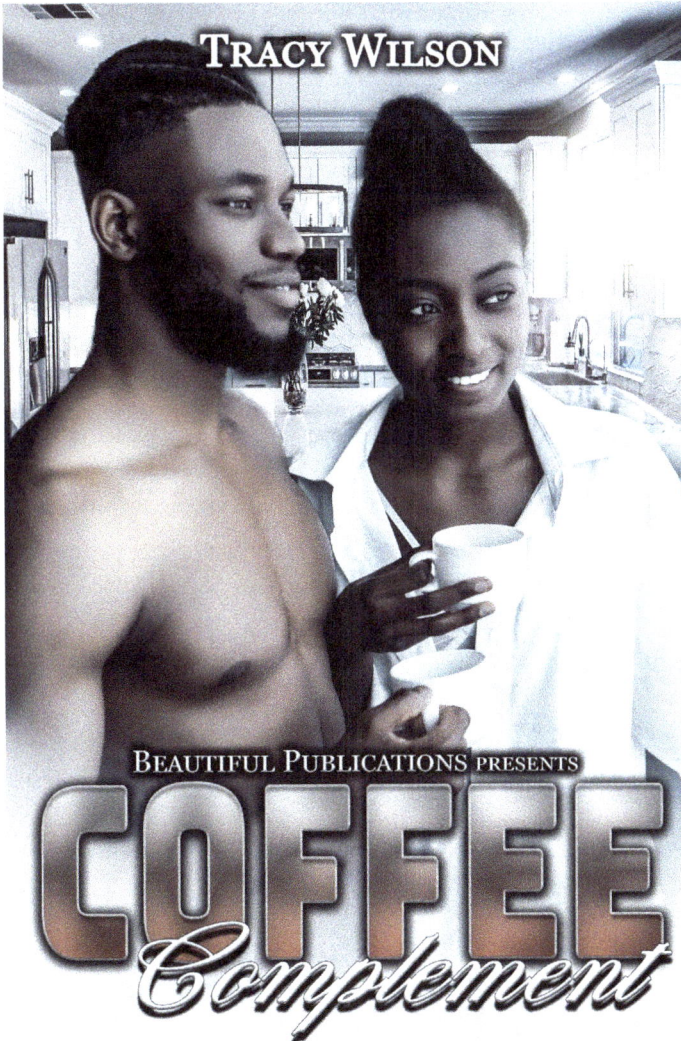

TRACY WILSON

BEAUTIFUL PUBLICATIONS PRESENTS

COFFEE
Complement

In 'In The Arms Of A Gangster,' Beautiee was given a pad & pencil to write with to help her deal with what was happening to her and how she was feeling while she was in jail and it led to her writing her autobiography.

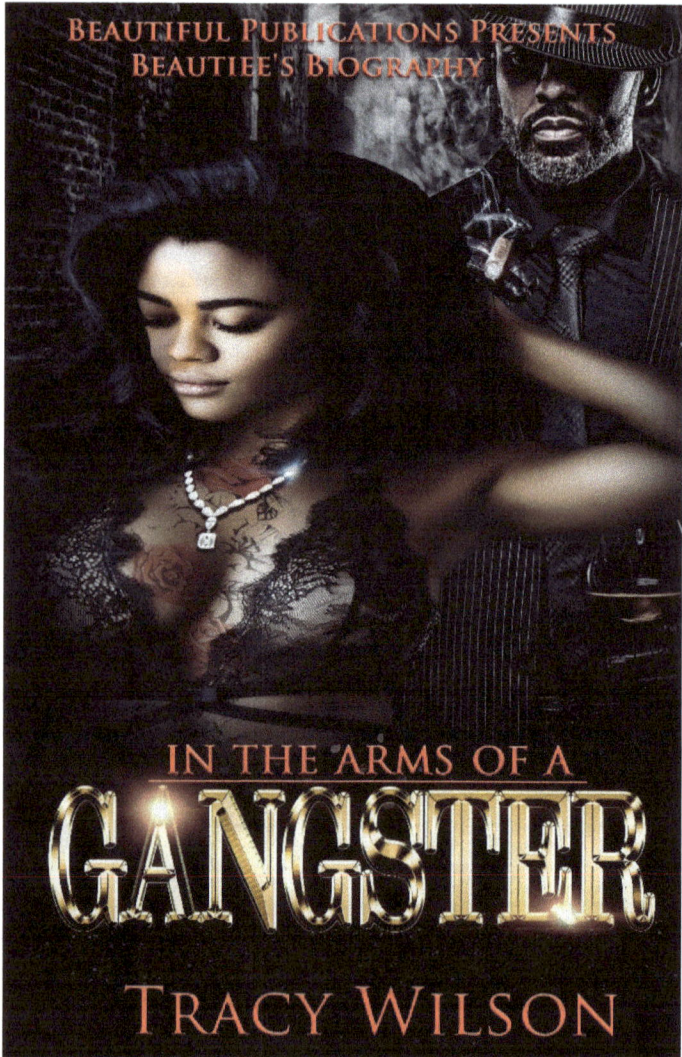

Do something fun with your children. My parents would sit at the table with coloring books and crayons and color with us and in the 'Twisted Series,' Bazil & Beautiee sat at the table and colored with their children. The 'Sweet Like Candy' series is a set of coloring books for adults made from my book covers.

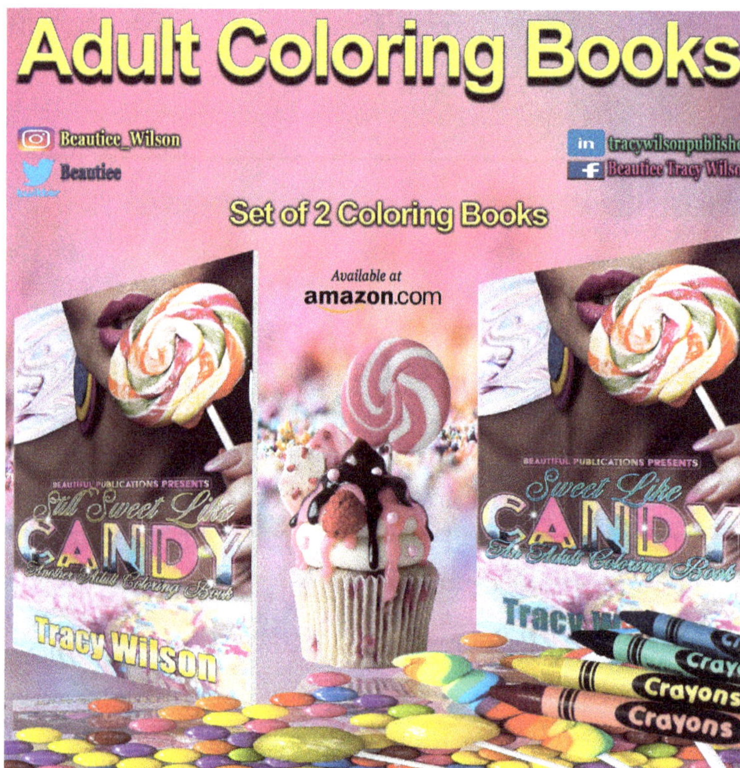
Adult Coloring Books
Beautice_Wilson
Beautiee
tracywilsonpublisher
Beautiee Tracy Wilson
Set of 2 Coloring Books
Available at
amazon.com
BEAUTIFUL PUBLICATIONS PRESENTS
Still Sweet Like
CANDY
Another Adult Coloring Book
Tracy Wilson
BEAUTIFUL PUBLICATIONS PRESENTS
Sweet Like
CANDY
The Adult Coloring Book
Crayons
Crayons

Another fun activity you can both do is get personal insight from my custom 'Urban Pearls Oracle Deck.' You can each pull a card and compare messages or you can take turns shuffling the deck to see if you both pull the same card.

AFTERWORD

Stay & Play Together is A Couples Guide To Longevity that includes real conversations, personal experiences, exercises, and examples from characters in my novels that have been through it all. I included pictures of my books because I wanted you to see the couples and imagine how they dealt with these issues. I hope you found this helpful.

Bibliography

1.   The modality (learning channel preference)
        questionnaire by O'Brien (1985), Stetson
        University, DeLand, FL

2.   Davis, Jeanie; Walton, Dominique, MD WebMD
        Feature "What's Great About Kissing" Stamford,
        Bryant, Ph.D. Health Promotion Center, University
        of Louisville; Davidson, Joy Ph.D. Psychologist &
        Clinical Sexologist, Seattle; Fisher, Helen, Ph.D.
        Professor of Anthropology, Rutgers University,
        Newark, New Jersey, 10/11/02

3.   Erotic Tori Present: "The Health Benefits of
        Orgasm!" Gorkin, Mark Sex Expert, Turner,
        Rebecca, MD San Francisco Medical Center,
        University of California, 10/11/02

4.   Kary, Tiffany, "Crying Over Spilled Semen."
        Psychology Today, Sep/Oct 2002, Vol. 35, Issue 5,
        p24, 1/2p, 10/11/02

5.   Blum, Jeffrey, Ph.D WebMD Feature "Can Good
        Sex Keep You Young?" Weeks, David MD, Old
        Age Psychology, Royal Edinburgh Hospital,
        Scotland; Meston, Cindy, M. Ph.D "Aging and
        Sexuality." Western Journal of Medicine" October
        1997; Love, Susan, MD; 10/11/02

6.   Bullough, Vern, L.; Bullough, Bonnie. "Human Sexuality – An Encyclopedia." Garland Publishing, Inc., New York & London 1994, pgs. 426, 427.

7.   Klein, Marty, Ph.D "Ask Me Anything" Question: I have read about people becoming sick from swallowing too much semen. How much is too much? http://www.sexed.org/askme/askme70.htlm, 10/11/02.

8.   Levine, Deb, MA "Ask the Experts" Question: When a man ejaculates, is it safe to swallow the semen? http://my.webmd.com/question_and_answer/article/1687.50117, 10/11/02

www.ingramcontent.com/pod-product-compliance
Lightning Source LLC
Chambersburg PA
CBHW071117090426

42736CB00031B/2474